*For all those who have encouraged
and inspired me*

Lincolnshire home

White hawthorn shines in springtime hedge
Red poppies blow on summer wold
Lime trees blaze out in autumn gold
Wind rustles in the winter sedge

Grey seas roll to endless empty sand
Green fens are still beneath the arching sky
Above the fields the lapwing's cry
This is our home, we are the land

Voices from the Vale

Poems

by

Ian Lacy

IronStone Books

12, Lime Grove, Cherry Willingham, Lincoln LN3 4BD

ISBN 978-0-99356723-2-3

Introduction

This second collection of poems most of which have been written over the last five years continues to explore the themes of *Lines from Lindsey:* landscape, life, love and faith. As I grow older, I increasingly realise that poetry really does reach parts of us that other words cannot reach, which perhaps explains why there is so much of it in the Bible. It enables us to explore and experiment in ways that can surprise, challenge, and delight us in ways "ordinary" words can struggle to do.

Poetry can also help us come to terms with loss and strengthen faith and hope. Some of these poems were written during the Covid-19 pandemic during 2020 and were an attempt to express how the tragedy affected my own thoughts and feelings, though I know that anything I experienced is minor when set against what so many have endured and indeed are still enduring.

It has helped me to have the blessing of being able to live in the Mid Lindsey Vale, a place which is "quiet and unobtrusive even by Lincolnshire standards" to quote Jon Fox in" The Lincolnshire Landscape - An Exploration" (Green Plover Books 2015) but has its own beauty and has been an inspiration to both the title of this collection and to many of the poems within it.

Contents

Voices in a time of Covid - 2020

Voices together

Voices of faith

Voices of the Seasons

Light on flooded dyke
Wind makes tall reeds sigh
Autumn edges towards dark

Mild day in January

Christmas past, reality now comes home.
Sombre clouds second the prevailing mood.
Our land. our lives face future set alone
Years of doubt for unclear long term good.
And coughs and colds, healthcare in disarray
A tide of debt, inflation, static pay
No homes to buy, true truth in sad retreat
Threats of snow, strikes and terror on the streets.

But. The air is mild, daylight now by eight.
Green crocus spears stab up from sodden soil
A distant blackbird tentatively sings.
First aconites glow golden by the gate.
Though cold return and rising hope recoil
After grey winter will come the green of spring.

Pause for lunch, February

Walking from Robin Hood's Bay to Ravenscar

Grateful we sit on sawn off branch
Two hours walk, ready to rest and eat
Well sheltered from the wind.
The forecast claimed it was winter's last rage
against the lengthening days.
Though the storm of Sunday's spiteful sleet
Is now mere bluster with no real power to harm.

Silence? No: the chatter of the beck
Hurrying down the shaded wyke
To meet the stern grey rollers of the sea.
A tiny whisper of protected air
Too faint to stir mossed branches
Or sway the last red holly berries.
And beyond the wood
Spring's first birds sing

From the sodden litter of fallen leaves
Green spears of daffodils are springing up
No buds yet, but sure promise of golden flowers
To sway in fresh March breeze.
A robin forages along the verge
A tiny insect takes to early flight.

Spring bike ride in the fens

New wheat shoots make a springtime sea of green
That shines like water under morning sun.
On either side the wooded slopes recede
As though we headed from an enclosed bight
To the wide oceans of the fens.

The quiet roads as surface currents take
Our bikes like boats that sail against the wind.
Farms, grey barns, church spires are reefs and islands
Homes for humanity to work and love,
Ports to hunt the harvest of the fen.

We go about and run downwind to home.
The friendly coasts draw in. And far ahead
The minster towers are leading marks by day
And lights by night to guide land sailors safe
Beneath the overarching sky.

Dawn Chorus

May. 4am. Lone blackbird starts to sing.
Defies darkness, cries joy to new day's light.
Ripples notes of hope, calls all live things
To celebrate the end of this long night.
Dawn chorus swells, though soon rooks' grating caws
Gives dark counterpoint to dream of hawthorn white
And wood pigeon's soft falling cadence swiftly cloys.

Dawn light grows. Birdsong begins to fade
Grey clouded sky claims only memory will last.
But as I turn to fall again to sleep
Blackbird's voice returns. Fresh new song is made
To prove life's melodies are not yet past.
New plans, new joys, new promises to keep.

June 30th 2016

The day before the 100th anniversary of the first day of the battle of the Somme

Last day of June.
Sharp cumulus in kingfisher sky
Marches briskly between Atlantic lows.
A late interval of summer to gladden hearts.

Hedgerows blossom.
Against green leaves dog roses softly glow
Late bridges from an unlamented spring
When endless rain fell on already sodden ground

Uncut verges.
Spear headed grass strains to steal advantage
Though gawky kexy's cream outreaches all.
In fields red poppies anticipate tomorrow's date.

Damp pasture smell.
Sweet honeysuckle's elusive tempting trace
Warm resin seeps from fresh cut weeping logs
Scents that yearn for longest days that have already passed.

The sound of birds.
Agitated flapping of wood pigeon wings.
A busy chatter over near-fledged broods.
And still above all the strained ascending song of larks.

Woodland shadow.
Straight tracks dappled by flickering shards of sun.
Pine and birch, doomed ash, still sturdy oak
Long lived beyond all that knows the gentle nurturing shade.

Beside the ruts
Foxglove purple bells. Brambles and clustered elderflower
Promise of autumn sweetness still to come
After harvest of summer hope. Then long winter's sleep.

Autumn Leaves

Late October. Long lasting summer fades
Into subdued shadows of northeast clouds.
Time turns back to old darkness before spring,
Long hours of evening gloom before the night.
Leaves now blaze faded green to red and gold
Then paling dry and blotch and curl and fall,
Reluctantly relinquish grip and spiral
Down to cooling hardening ground below
Where for a time they rustle, shift, before
Inevitable incorporation into earth.

And I – in the October of my life –
Ask if the green hopes that in spring once showed
And grew into a semblance of maturity
But dulled with usage in the years since then
May yet still turn in autumn's final fling
To russet, gold, bring last glorious colour
To shortening days before the winter comes.
Before, pried loose from long familiar branch
They flutter, graceful fall to lie awhile
Perhaps bring pleasure to small scuffling feet.

Or has autumn glory already faded,
Slipping, soundless, soft to sad sodden soil?
Colour, form and texture lost to become
Litter that that browns the winter woodland floor
Unmarked among ten million more
Whose falling reveals the bare fractal frame.
Trunks, branches, twigs. Societal structure
Deep roots in time, slow built by all the years
Of long forgotten joyous springtime leaves
Who unfolding loved, gave life then fading, died.

Latrigg – January 2017

Latrigg is the hill that overlooks Keswick, under the shadow of Skiddaw

Winter fells against a winter sky
Snow slopes merge with coldest blue
Bright chill air, remote high wisps of cloud.
Summits softened as the year dissolves
Set limits to chill dale's still shadowed ground.

Enfolded by the outreaching riggs
Brown bracken, still golden birch
Hold faded traces of a summer lost.
The grey town, quiet, roofs still white with frost
That lingers. Dreams slow melting into time

Gentle cold-fingered wind whispers loss,
Stirs blades of diamonded grass
That with bright short noon will lose their spark
And merge with earth in falling dusk forgotten.
Black hills and stars remain against the dark.

Witham Winter - Dusk

Air, water, earth, icefire.

Boundary between fen wapentakes.

Current slow flows east, then south to sea.

Ducks' alarmed flight ripples silver against the grey.

Edging reeds sough in cold northern wind.

Far off, the minster silhouette above the river gap.

Grey clouds touched pale against the fading sky.

Harsh single croak of solitary crow.

Ice lies thin along the water edge.

Just four o'clock: day is almost done.

Kicked mounds of questing hungry moles.

Light fades shades of green to brown, then grey.

Mute swans slow on surface of the delph.

Noise of homebound children fades, tree hidden across the flow.

Over all the infinity of Lindsey sky.

Pockets of last week's fall of snow in high bank's shadow.

Quiet now. All small birds have gone to roost.

Reflections brief return as ruffled water stills.

Trees, bare boned black against the coming night.

Underfoot, whispering boots on frosted grass.

Vapour trails catch light from westered sun.

Willows now outlined black against the darkening fields

Extend their sad branches to the dying year.

Yearn for spring. But this season has its treasures too.

Zone between seasons, dark and light, here and further bank.

Running in the Mist

Mist. Not dream drawn summer vapour from the river
That vanishes with rising of the sun.
But creeping, damp, chilled from cold wet earth
Seeping upward into low hanging clouds.
Constricting vision, blurring shape and shade
Confusing sound to directionless grey noise
Condoning loss of purpose, progress, pace
Confirming that the fading light will die.

I know this place, each fading formless hedge.
The rise and fall of shadowed slope and path.
The turns, iced ruts, last seasons frosted stubble.
For I have run this darkening route before
And know in spring those hawthorn hedges bloom
And ruts reflect the soft blue sky.

Voices from the past

Long-ago lives speak
To our so different world
Love, hope, do not change

Psalm 84 v3

"Even the sparrow has found a home and the swallow a nest for herself where she may have her young- a place near your altar Lord Almighty ,my King and my God"

Spring. Swallows swoop, home once more
from winter a continent away
seeing in their guided flight
wonders which no pilgrims here
have looked on or imagined in their dreams.
Small insect life, swept up from valley far below
breeze-borne food for them around
the man-built cliffs of sun-warmed stone
built as home for (though it cannot hold)
God whose praises upwards swirl
past mud-built nests, secure beneath the eaves.

Warm flagstones. Sparrows squabbling
glean offered grain, fallen as it was waved.
Not travellers, they know each corner
that is safe from keen eyed kestrel
or merlin's heart stopping stoop to seize and kill.
They also know their market two a farthing worth
but are still content to be about
the bronze gates of this special place
where the Maker of stone, bird and man
is loved, worshipped and obeyed
The longed-for place of swallow, sparrow, me.

Isaiah c7

The prophet looks back on the message he has given to King Ahaz. The King had refused to ask for a sign to confirm God's promise of rescue from the clear and present danger of invasion, but God promises a child will be born.

I sit. Think back to this day's dawn.
The message that came into my mind from God
(to whom alone be praise and glory).
I walked quiet streets, smelt the sickly fear,
rumour of invading army drawing near.

I found the king where God had said.
The confrontation that I knew would come
(for he is arrogant and afraid).
The politics of cunning blindness,
flat refusal of God's loving-kindness.

Hope beyond all your "common sense."
Dread enemies will vanish like a dream
(God is in ultimate control).
Challenges beyond but still the living Lord
who will bring peace: believe his promised word.

And when the king, refusing sign,
showed contempt for God's far greater power
(false piety of fallen man),
the Spirit's voice moved within me, cried
`'A young woman will conceive and bear a child"

Before his birth the threat is gone.
His mother knows that he will grow up safe
(she –joyful - names him "God with us").
Before his wisdom's grown northlands are laid waste
Judah in greater danger than it has ever faced.

As I think on what I said this day
ideas elusive as the gentle breeze
(hints of greater truth to come in time?).
What if God were truly to be with us
To remake his world, his people, glorious?

What would it mean, our God made man,
yet still be God, self-limited by love?
(it seems so near blasphemy and yet...)
Back in the joyous garden before sin
lost us our peace, our evening walk with him?

What would the world be if the power
of the Most High Lord should flood our darkness?
The Light dazzling making blind eyes see?
Sin's night defeated and all things made new,
A child's life among us who was God's presence too?

How could it be, unless, unless...
in some way that child who would one day be born
(a virgin birth? God is above all)
should be both God and perfect sacrifice
to die and then as new dayspring arise.

I, Isaiah. king's counsellor
proclaim truth to those who do not want to hear
(though this truth is given me by God).
I speak more than I can in this life know.
What God has promised he will in grace bestow.

Mary

Spring morning light Dew-sparkled grass
as I lift the empty jar and walk
steeply down between shadowed houses
to the well. I'm early. Glad today
there are only smiles, quiet greetings,
not the teasing, comments, knowing looks
from those who mock and envy joy.
Betrothal to an older man.
They do not know his caring kindness,
his gentle smile, confidence, calm skill.
Jar filled, I turn uphill for home,
tasks of an ordinary day.

Summer afternoon. Dry Judean hills.
I rest, the slight nausea has gone.
Inside, Elizabeth's calm slow steps,
careful of her coming child and me.
Safe from gossip, faces turned away,
I think of that ordinary morn,
ending in a way I still cannot
fully comprehend. Angel's words
that put me on a path not travelled
before. Yet I know essential truth.
The child within me, still too small
to feel, yet more than any child has been.
So when I said "God's will be done,"
history changed. God is in me.

Cool autumn evening. Sunset's afterglow.
My wedding day. Not young girl's glory
I dreamt last year. None there save those who
had to be. My swelling body hid
by new blue cloak, his wedding gift to me.
Dear Joseph, so concerned to do right
by law, by promise and by me.
He knows the full true state of things.
He too met Gabriel, in the dark
of dreams. He too heard the will of God.
Accepting that, accepted me
and now sleeps sound. The child within me stirs.

Cold winter night. Frost sharp outside.
The stars look down, windows of the world
from which this sleeping baby came.
Now close wrapped, warm, safe in scented hay.
He watched wide eyed the shepherds' kneeling forms.
Heard the soft swish of cattle stirring straw.
Cried briefly, fed and closed his eyes
on this dark world to which he's come.
I, nine months of wonder, brief hour of pain
forgotten in joy this child is born.
I sense sadness in time to come.
For this moment he is mine alone.

Joseph's Prayer

"Lines from Lindsey" has a poem called Joseph's Joy – this is a more sombre version of Joseph's thoughts and prayers when he discovered Mary was pregnant before their marriage.

Lord, I do not understand.
My hopes dashed, my joy destroyed.
The girl I love, dishonoured and unchaste.
What am I to do, Lord
to cross the empty waste
of life stretched out in loss and grief and shame?

Lord, I know what I must do.
Reduce the risk of Mary's shame.
The girl I love: a quiet place, remote, safe.
But what should I do, Lord
To keep that poor sad waif
his life mapped out for scorn and hate and pain?

Lord, I start to understand.
An angel spoke, my joy restored.
The girl I love: mother of Messiah
I will protect and care
For both through snow and fire.
Lives shining out in love and hope and peace.

Wilderness

What were they like, those forty days alone?
The noise of crowd faded on Jordan's bank.
The still hot air of desert afternoon
Air shimmering, all but you asleep

What was in your mind and heart?
Memories of your childhood home?
Nazareth, timber, chisels and the lathe
The family you left for these hard stones?

The words of Cousin John, who baptised you
the dove's descent, your father's voice above?
Crowd briefly silent as you walked away to this.
Hunger, heat, temptation to conform.

Shepherd, you surveyed the land you'd lead through.
Healer, you experienced pain.
King, you triumphed over evil.
Short cuts that would have bypassed your cross.

Yes, you thought through the words about you.
Yes, meditated on the Word you are.
Yes, the future as it lay before you.
Yes, the knowledge of the death you'd die

More. You prayed beyond the next three years.
Looking to those who would one day believe
in times and lands you made and are still making.
Including – love so incredible – me.

The woman at the well

Dawn. Dim light brings shape to this familiar room.
He stirs. I lie, waiting soft footfalls, sleepy voices
heading down to the gate, the well beyond.
I recall when I could freely go.
Join the greetings, the chat, the friendly tease.
Together in life's rhythm: to care, to be, to love.

Morning. I rise, draw yesterday's warm stale water
from that jar whose carried shade I use to hide my face
in pointless search to be no longer me.
Fit for purpose but flat and dead.
Weary, I fan the sulky embers to a flame.
Enough for bread and being, but not enough for life.

Noon. Harsh light. Colour flattened to dull haze by glare.
The town quiet. Tasks laid down. Baby in dark doorway cries.
I slip between shadows. Afraid.
Though I know from long experience
there will be nothing worse than silence.
Averted eyes. Not even gossip. My feet stir the dust.

At the well's rim the sun strikes. Cracked dry mud edge curled,
breaking into dust that is all there is in me.
This morning water splashed, jokes and secrets shared. Friends.
The jar set down. Reluctant to start
a task that will send me back to where I was.
Then a man. Alone. A Jew. Asking for water.

Afternoon. Shadows soften. I am speaking. No!
Crying out! Excited! Hope filled! Understood!
For that man, that Jew, told me all I'd done
but did not condemn me.
Treated me as human, answered questions.
Challenged. Cared. And told me who he was. With love.

Evening. The dark comes. But not as yesterday. Lonely guilt.
Defiance. Now neighbours flood the lamplit room.
New friends who smile. Whom I have linked to him.
They too know he is Messiah.
Hope is here. Questions remain. How could these short hours
tell all he is, all he promises for us?

Night. I lie awake. Nothing new but not like this.
Looking forward. Words linger. Such gentle words. Direct.
But mercy for me. Lost, now found. New day.
New life. Forgiven for the past.
And though I love my man and will so still
Yet I love too this man who cares. Smiles. Heals. Restores.

Voices from life

Aircraft engine thunder fades
Once more a lone blackbird sings
He was always there

Summer Night, Cornwall

C. S. Lewis's "The Discarded Image" explains the mediaeval world view of humankind as confined to the innermost sphere of creation, (limited by the orbit of the moon), excluded by the fall –our own choices – from full participation in the music of the spheres. A few nights after reading it I saw the lights of Boscastle across the moonlit bay

Soft summer night. I stand above the bay.
Silvered horizon, the moon's distorted track
Reflecting boundary between this sphere and the next.
Folds of different darkness shadowed at my feet.
Drowsed roar of surf on broken cliffs beneath.

Across the bay village lights speak friends,
Homes, warm bodies merged in love.
It's true that I could walk the darkened lanes,
Risk unseen briars, stumbling in the now black grass.
But it would take time. Lights go out
And sleep cuts off that good world from my reach.

I turn and look above. The stars are village lights
A haven cut off by vasts of time and space.
Are they too partners in a dance of life,
Complex joy of satisfied desire
Singing music beyond range of human ear?

Suppose my reference point was not myself
Sea, village, stars defined by where I stand?
So I no longer gazed across a void,
Missing songs in which I cannot join.
Suppose I were already in the dance?

Then I would know this sphere is my true living space.
Understand that what lies out there is real.
That I am no lost stranger here,
Outside the wall, cut off by all past choices
From dancing rhythm, the beauty of those voices.

Could I then stay as I am? Self-denied my place.
Self-condemned to darkness, refusing grace,
A way across the boundaries of the spheres
To starlight music that denies the void,
To village firelight love to be enjoyed.

Referendum Eve 8pm

Deep cloud shuts off all view
Of wider, clearer skies.
Silence of summer air cuts all
Sound but that of birds and ticking clocks
And quiet voices outside the village hall.

Past and future are now remade.
It is right the air is still,
No hint of where the breeze will blow.
How choice will shape our children's lives,
Our own and where this silent land will go.

Harsh words, half-truths now fade and die
With graphs, guesses, experts,
Before the verdict we now give
Bringing on ourselves our fate.
But now stillness. Tomorrow a new start.

Three sonnets at Port en Alls

The first sonnet was inspired by a prolonged flash of reflected light on the Lizard across Mounts Bay , seen from Port en Alls (Prussia Bay, near Marazion in Cornwall) as all else faded into haze. The third the result of the following morning's sunlight, and then, some weeks later, I wrote the nocturne

I - Dusk

To eastward curve of coast fades into haze
Shape, colours swallowed in uncertainty
Of where land, sea, sky keep identity
Separate from each other. This dying day's
Light now merges with growing dark that lays
Night on prospects of bright eternity
With loss of all in greyed infinity.
And we can only long this sad moment stays.
But from the grey strikes point diamond light
Reflected from that other truth, the sun
Answering life's thin thread is not yet spun.
Hope beyond darkness of the coming night
Dawn in the east will yet make all things right
Bright present proof of new day yet to come.

II - Night

Night. Uneasy dark lies dull across the sea
Pressing down the weight of all men's doubt.
All forms that make life sure the mist blots out
Though by day it merely speaks of mystery.
No air soft stirs a leaf of summer tree.
Only the endless tidal rise and fall
Sighs on sand. No mournful night birds call
Their plaintive news of when the dawn may be.
And then long miles away a lighthouse gleam
Man-made brief flash of hope against the dark.
Enough to steer a course against the stream.
Enough to show good men may make their mark,
Proclaim bright day to come beyond the dream
And rise with courage skyward as the lark.

III - Morning

New morning and across the sweeping bay
What was lost in mist is now made plain.
The lines of cliff sea chaos still restrain
That men may wake and go about their day
Encouraged to labour, love and play.
In homes and fields warm summer comes again
Surety of harvest, soon ripening grain
Stored 'gainst winter in firm-built barn will lay.
Last night's fears now seem small but no less real
Those truths of empty death that all men dread
Lightless pathways we know are ours to tread
Though now our little lives seem strong as steel.
But – light has come. Whatever lies ahead
Cannot dismay those whose hope is not yet dead.

Questioning the winds

"Where do you come from, southwest wind
Sharp raindrops fresh against my face?"
"From Atlantic deeps, past the Azores.
Across Cornish cliffs and Devon moors,
Up Severn's stream, past Newark town
Soaking fields, ploughed, furrowed, brown."

"Where do you come from, northeast wind
Stinging sleet against bowed head?"
"From taiga, tundra, cold Zemlya's lea
Norway's snow mountains, wave grey North Sea.
Marram dunes, marsh and windswept wold
Bleak bringer of deep dark and cold."

"Where do you come from, northwest wind
Sweeping storm clouds across the stars?"
"From far Ellesmere Land, the elder ice.
Greenland glaciers, lone Hirta's height,
Glasgow slate rooftops, Pennine fells
Calling adventure, weaving spells."

"Where do you come from, southeast wind
Touching gentle on my cheek?"
Arabian desert, Danube plain,
Moselle vineyards, chalkland terrain.
Essex creeks, woods, fertile fen
Breathing warm summer's come again."

Feeding the hens
(The Beast from the East, 2018)

Wind hurled snow stings faces
Powder clogs the hidden track.
Trees moan. Grey light.
Last day of winter.

Frozen bolt chills fingers
Fumble opening the gate.
Hens cluster round
Unfazed by storm.

Warm feathers against white
Wattles cheerful red in gloom
Corn pecked as if
This was a summer day.

A short walk home. We worry.
Will we cope, 3 days alone?
Stay warm and fed?
Hens don't fret.

Just live from day to day
Confident they will be fed.
We know that too.
So why concerned?

Park Run

The lean lithe club runners for whom 5k
Is merely light relief on Saturday.
The unfit overweight who simply just
Long to lose pounds because they know they must.
The young, the old, the work-worn middle aged,
School children who have all week been caged.
First timers worrying "Will I get around?"
Regulars well knowing familiar ground.
Sleek buggies powered by long limbed super mums,
Dogs secret thinking this is no real run.

We clap the volunteers and visitors
Who add to their collection this flat course.
"Let's run'" The surge across to starting line.
"Hi there! Good luck! Run well! You'll be just fine."
The countdown from three ends in a scuff,
Eight hundred coloured trainers pounding off.
Legs stretching to their full potential length
(more training will yet improve their latent strength).
Adjustment jostle round the path side seat
The slow fall back, the fit are running fleet.

Across the narrow bridge the dense crowd thins
As now for some the serious run begins.
Others regret their wild ambitious start
And briefly fear for their now straining heart.
The back straight now, carefully avoiding those
Who walk contrary wise and seem to doze.

Through wooded glade: no slippery leaves
Excuse a pause for those whose tight chests heave.
Then narrow path where some first fool a stitch
Others go wide, risk falling in the ditch.

Now the second lap. The thundering herd
Sweep by fluorescent marshals who applaud
And then prepare, for in twelve minutes time
The swiftest will approach the finish line
While the rest, mere mortals, keep up the slog
Some run, some walk, some manage a slow jog.
So what? This is meant to be at least some fun
Summer Saturday warmed by morning sun
Though some now think that stopping's best of all
Like ceasing to bang head against brick wall.

Lap three. And now the faster overtake
Those slower souls who've not yet passed the lake.
They too are still giving it their best
Though moist of brow and sweaty under vest.
Last time through woodland and the welcome turn
Homewards tired as legs, once just aching, burn.
Slight downhill gives last chance to quicken stride
A final burst of speed at least is tried.
At last the funnel's final fond embrace
Past the timer and we can slacken pace.
The plastic tokens are in order given
We stop, gasp and enter Park Run heaven.

Lincoln Park Runners will recognise the 3-lap run round Boultham Park

Voices in a time of Covid, 2020

Quiet sunlit roads
Sad fear presses down
Wheat grows, sure hope of harvest

The seed is sown

"Only go outside for food, health reasons or work"

Roads run strangely silent under March spring blue sky
Bright sun but clear air holds winter chill
Fields that should be inches high with green
Sodden, threaten summer will have to pass them by.

Isolated driver, too fast to see his face
(Why rush? Home's the only place to go)
Cyclist passes me the other way
Raised hand, "Hello" across at least two metres space.

Across the low hedge, slow sailing the field's brown sea
Red tractor, hopper full of seed
Precision planting hopeful earth
Harvest promise for when this spring is memory.

The wheat breaks through

Seven weeks since small seeds
Sank into the waiting soil's embrace.
Seven weeks of waiting. Life suspended.
Sickness, anger, death, argument and loss.
Quiet roads, queues, sorrow under empty skies,
Rainbows, brave faces, Thursday cheers to give
Our weary selves assurance we still live.

Now these seeds, so late sown
In the final chance of late March earth
Are green, inching high, straining to the light
Of May. Smiled on by white hawthorn bloom
Fragrant beneath the blue of Lindsey's sky.
Blackbird sings, though eastern breeze blows chill
Reminder pandemic is with us still.

But there is promise. Harvest will yet come.
We shall meet again, warmed by summer sun.

The wheat grows tall

Midsummer now. The wheat stands stiff and straight.
Grey turns green as clouds hide, then clear the sun.
Twenty million upright unripe ears.
Ninety growing days from small seeds sown.
Ninety-one since this pandemic time began.
Reality of numbers. No stray weeds
Of wistful imaginations' fantasies.
Hard facts. Hard grain. Existence. Basic needs.

Down the road the soft barley lilting sways.
Greensilver rippled by the gentlest breeze.
Whispering soft, caressing the bare legs
Of those who slip between new growth and the hedge.
Poppy blushed, flower of joy and loss and hope.
Barley becomes beer, malt loaf, cattle feed.
To bring us milk, beef in long months to come.
Good things add life to basic being's creed.

The wheat nears harvest

Waiting. Short spell of summer sun
Will change bleached gold to full firm yellow glow.
Waiting. Summer rain's brief kiss. Sweet
To swell tall heads and weight them gently down.
Waiting. For others to decide
The moment that is death and life for wheat.

Death. What this wheat was planted for.
Not to joy eye, ear by beauty.
Death. Not lingering, clinging on
Till autumn, winter frost's decay and rot.
Death then would give no purpose but
To be ploughed to earth, first fine promise gone.

Life. Rolling combine's circling sweep.
Cut, threshed, then ground, kneaded, raised and baked.
Life. Not re-incarnate grain
But transformed to bring to sad world anew
The bread of life and hope and joy
Sown, grown, cut down and raised to live again.

Harvest begins

Not the weather farmers hope for.
Not sun with gentle night-time rain
That gives the final swelling to the grain

But cloudy skies and blustering gales
Breaking branches, flattening corn
Promised change betrayed by yet new storm.

Not the summer we had wanted
Freed from fear, hard pandemic past.
Mourn, move on, life once more within our grasp.

But disease tide so slow ebbing
Restrictions for the common good
Endless arguments over "must "and "should."

Now at last the combine's moving
Grain pours into open trailer
Yield down, yes, but not a total failure.

Shops are open, lovers freely meet
Cautious holidays, seaside trip
Surely starting to escape this evil's grip?

Hard to think back to springtime sorrow
Harsh statistics, the News at Ten.
God in mercy, let it not come again.

After the harvest

Late September. The empty field
Lies quiet beneath the autumn sky.
Gold stubble fades to washed out straw
Shadowed by hedges, their final green
Splashed with red of hips, haws and bramble black
Spring's flowered promises fulfilled

Even the bales, bound by-products gone,
Leaving space, a soft short interval of peace
To think on these last six months past.
The fear, the caring unity
Now cut down like wheat. Urgent moving on.
Resume, renew, get back to work
Now the economy comes first

But think of those who like this field
Are bounded by the barrier of a hedge
Alive but empty at their heart.
Who shop, pay bills, go on from day to day
Mourning for unexpected death,
Or caring souls, cut down by prolonged pain
Or lonely, cannot understand.

No consolation, for now their loss
Has been subsumed within the greater good.
All lives are but a bottom line
To plough, sow, reap, to make still bigger fields.
Must Christ die in every generation
To enrich those without imagination?

The field in late winter

It snowed last night, whitening unploughed stubble
Hiding tired grass faded by long winter gloom
Clinging briefly to dead bramble stems
Ghost memories of normal life
From summer past

Low grey clouds press down on naked hedgerow trees
Twigs scratch fragmented patterns above sad earth
Lonely crow flies slow from east to west
Tired wind stirs cold from wolds and sea.
One more drear day

But look more closely. In depths of snow melt hedge
Thin buds tentatively reaching to the light
On field's far side a blackbird calls
Another faintly answers him
Spring is waking

Ten months have gone since seeds were sown. Sadness grew.
Grief, weariness, broken hopes. Suspended lives.
Loss beyond our worst imagining.
Empty schools, shops, TV-side chairs
Covid 19

Coda: Duty doctor at the Covid 19 vaccination clinic

This sun-streaked January afternoon
I am the duty doctor.
Come back to the pandemic present
To be a sort of gallery curator
Watching vaccinated patients
For something I hope will never happen.
Observing for reactions, waiting for calls to help

These old faces who wait out their fifteen minutes
Have moved from imposed isolation's room
Into a passageway that will lead
To windowed waiting place where they can view
Grey winter's Covid sullen grip
Become daffodils, spring's soft free air
Though February's sad news and setbacks are to come.

A year stolen from lives that will live less long
Than full years already lived.
And long to hold, be held by those they love
The experts do not yet know when this will end.
Each now leaves, grateful, tentative
Stepping out the door to go back home
Still patient but planning hope, the picking up of threads.

Nineteen months have passed
Another harvest, come, gone
Autumn tears still flow
                    November 2021

Voices together

Outside cold darkness
Inside candlelight
Falling softly on your breast

We two alone

Grammatically, you cannot really say
"we two alone."
It is almost an oxymoron,
for alone means one.
And though in common speech the phrase
is used to shut out and defy the world,
alone is at heart solitary,
a lost and longing word.
But we two who apart were once alone have now become
one together in each other's love.
One found self, though still two who share
a single joyous place
where we two are one
But not alone.

The new kitchen

When, new married, we first ate together
We sat facing, so eyes could meet the other's gaze
Across the novelty of shared breakfast table.
Now committed and discovering each other's lives.

When children came, we sat at meals together
Four chairs right angled, across from daughter, son.
Cereal, spread on toast, marmalade and tea
Eyes on the clock, another working day.

And when they left, launched out into the world
We kept on sitting in our habitual place
Sharing quiet before separate days ahead,
A partnership, joint but several space.

But now in these present late glad memory times
No corners come between, we now sit side by side
Sharing sunlight on morning garden, birdsong, trees
A day together, joy then blessed night.

Saturday

"Flesh and blood needs flesh and blood and you're the one I need"
Johnny Cash

We spent the afternoon apart
Though bounded by the fence of our created world
Where we (ignoring inconveniences like rain)
Looked to ripening of ideas and plans and hopes.
You, tired from listening to the night of lost and sad
Engrossed in reading of a past time
Where good men believing crushed each other's dreams.
I, patching a roof where insinuating damp
Had crept like old age through unregulated gaps
And pruning branches that, uncontrolled in youth,
Obstruct the light that should ripen autumn fruit.

And then the fireside warmth.
Light white wine, sparkling hint in tall -stemmed glass.
Chicken, rice, tomatoes with memory of south summer sun.
Music, a film and then the touch of lips
The holding, the ache of joy, the being one.
For though we each need our solitary space
It is shaped by years of life and love
And cannot be truly filled except by giving each to both.
So now we turn to sleep: twin-starred centre
Of our life's orbit, turning in darkness.
The void beyond is cold but patterned by the stars.

Summit

On this high hill
That overtops all peaks on the long ridge ahead
We take time to rest, renew ourselves,
To look back down the long climbing path
Some turns now hidden, others in held view,
That we have climbed together through these years.
And see the shadowed parts were only under clouds
That passed with wind and time
Over sunlit meadows and the friendly shade of trees
Past joys, hopes and dreams fulfilled.

We turn away from this wide view
And see once more each other.
Friends, companions, travellers on the way
Bodies more prone to tiredness than once perhaps they were
But love still fresh as when we began this walk.
No words. We smile, touch hands
And side by side move on.

Anniversary

The years have passed.
Dreams fulfilled and dreamt anew.
The threefold cord whose strands began to weave
When first we held each other in tentative embrace
Has grown stronger as storm and sun
Tightened the multiplying strands
And now makes secure all that we once pledged.
Lives shared so each to other still can give
Joy, hope and friendship
That will endure as long as love shall live.

The still beauty
Of your sleeping smile
More lovely than the southern stars

Seasons of our love

Once there was winter.
The cold dark time before we met.
A heart empty ache
Unrecognised perhaps and yet
A sense that some time
We'd say to someone "I am yours."

Then there was springtime.
Bright daffodils against blue sky.
Hands held, laughing lips,
Certain that both in each have joy.
A life together
Knowing, trusting, gentle caring.

After that came summer.
Long days of green, hills, sparkling sea.
The children growing,
Becoming themselves as we
Explored through sun, tears
The heights, the depth, the breadth of love

Now it is autumn.
Leaves blaze red, gold before they fall.
Our love, now older,
Stronger, more part of us with time.
No fears of winter.
Lives so made one will never part.

Voices of faith

Despite the dark clouds
Christmas gives hope to memory
Glory glimpsed through gap

Rooted

"that you, being rooted and grounded in love may have power together with all the saints, to grasp how wide and deep and high and deep is the love of Christ ,and to know this love that surpasses knowledge – that you may be filled with all the fulness of Christ."
Ephesians c3 v17-19

Rooted in dark embrace of earth
Safe from cold winter's overlay
The first faint stirring of reviving life
Pale buds push upwards to new birth

Grounded in richness of good soil
Provided with the needs for growth
Rain of grace seeps down to nourish hope
That no return of frost can spoil

Season moves on to early spring
Shoots break through into a wider world
Green, tentative but stretching to the sky
Where clouds scud by and skylarks sing

Stems grow and swell to latent bloom
Aware that what they will become
Is more than this, their true and destined self
Dancing joyful after winter's gloom.

One day of warmth beneath blue sky
The sleepers wake to gold and glory
And know surpassing love that unlike earth's
Daffodils will not fade and die

The chapterhouse

Written in the chapter house of Lincoln Cathedral whilst acting as a steward for the Methodist Collection of Modern Art "Passion in Paint" exhibition, Lent 2016

Faint footsteps die soft on echoing stone
The quiet drops down from arches apex gloom
Dim light through coloured glass pervades the room.
Sighing round the towers the wind's faint moan,
Outside the hungry weekday traffic's drone
Underscores the silence as do the tombs
That lie beneath the stones. The common doom
Of those who served here and now sleep alone.

As we are with our thoughts, our fears, our dreams
Temporary guardians of this place
Surrounded by pictures that speak God's grace
That flows from deep love as quiet streams
From depths well up and would all life embrace
And in silence speak to us face to face.

Garden in the gale

Blown, blustered, battered.
Trees wind bent, almost breaking
Under the pressure of late May gale
Still beautiful? I made it.

The church in our land
Tossed by storms that strike our life
Incessant since times before recall
Still beautiful? He shaped it.

Science. Northern blast
Claiming all is chance plus time.
Only what is measurable is true.
Stark facts. Truth without joy.

Reason. Western wind.
Progress cancels out the past.
Only what we can think is true.
Deep thoughts. Dust without life.

One-ness. Eastern gust.
All is but a single whole.
Life force alone. No One there to know.
Blind fate. Stars without hope.

Post - truth. Southern breeze.
We can be what we desire.
Real is merely how we want to feel
Fulfilled. Mist without dawn.

Our shape distorted.
Swayed by the world wild winds
We offer weak words blown away.
Doctor. First be healed.

Laws of logic without love.
Desires uncorrected by the Word.
Love held separate to holiness.
Emotion substituting truth.

But still the Gardener
Comes with mercy to his own.
Repairs, restores, replants life truth.
Still beautiful. He loves her.

A158

(The road to the coast)

Summer Sunday morning and the traffic's flowing east
Away from the cathedral and the celebration of old feasts.
Past fields and wolds and woodlands and little wayside chapels
To sea and sand and burgers, the taste of toffee apples.

Summer Sunday lunchtime and the road is empty to the coast
The day visitors eat sandwiches, the homestayers eat roast
Making family conversation and sharing on their phone
The new pictures of the children so they won't feel alone.

Summer Sunday evening and the traffic's flowing west
To back up on the bypass and undo the weekend's rest
Skin suntanned, sand in shoes and minds and bodies tired
Eyes can no longer see the minster towers reach skyward.

Chapel Closure

"The cause has failed" is the traditional Methodism phrase sometimes used when the decision is taken to close a chapel. The first lines are a quote from Matthew Arnold's great poem about loss of faith, "Dover Beach".

You could see it as the sad small grating of pebbles
That amplified to near infinity
Make the melancholy withdrawing roar
Of faith into the dark of history.

You could see it as the closing of a store.
No demand in a changed economy.
Not profitable, draining resources
That could shore up a failing cause elsewhere.

You could see it as reason's latest triumph
Driving belief into the black void of
Meaninglessness that is this universe
Now revealed and properly understood.

You could see it as secular hammer blow
To intolerant old ways that pour guilt
On bright experience of liberated souls
Who can create their heaven on this earth.

But you would be wrong. Tides turn and flood once more.
Brands may change but all still need the food.
Reason's cold light shows up our inner dark.
Dead hammered bodies rise again to life.

Restoration

Destroyed buildings
Broken roads
Detritus of self-inflicted war
Revolt broken
Resistance at an end
We wait the coming of the king.

Debt burden
Labour hard
Obligation bound
Rations, no more
Permitted to survive
We wait the justice of the king.

Left alone
Written off
Scrabbling for bare crust
No rights to claim
No hope, no joy, no peace
We wait the anger of the king.

What is this?
A gentle smile?
Hands stretched out in love
Give back our peace
Ransom, healing, restoration.
We take the free grace of the King

The new Ulysses

"To strive, to seek, to find and not to yield"

Alfred, Lord Tennyson: "Ulysses"

"But one thing I do: forgetting what is behind and straining towards what is ahead, I press on towards the goal to win the prize for which God has called me heavenwards in Christ Jesus"

Paul, Philippians c 3 vs 13-14

To start out again when comfort calls and
Strive to do new things while continuing
To work on the old so as to
Seek to surpass the best that I have done before.
To relearn the joy of just being and to
Find that joy in the everyday things
And allow long love to ripen into autumn beauty
Not shrivel in the early frosts.
To learn to accept limitations but not to
Yield to tempting softness of the armchair of age.
For:
There are higher mountains still **to**
Climb. More "best evers" to **strive**
To reach. More poems still **to**
Write, more good knowledge still to **seek.**
So it is necessary to journey on **to**
Unexpected waypoints and **find**
They are the start of new adventures **and**
Bring new joys that will **not**
Fade into grey dusk as I come **to**
See older age as challenge, not a call to **yield.**

Return to Lindisfarne

We left the isle at dusk (ebb tide made easy
The natural forgetting of our home)
To chase the promise of the setting sun
In a far country beyond dark enticing hills.

Through springtime green, though drenched at times by tears,
Summer's bright fulness, following the flow.
Sharp light of autumn, slow decay of dreams.
Winter's chill message: all earth light must fade.

Until we turned and crossed again the sand
Heading back before flood tide wiped away
The footsteps of our passing. Facing east
We walked towards the ever-rising Son
Whose love till then unknown
Had yet guided us to bring us home.

Christmas Eve, 2020

When I was a GP the drive home from the surgery on Christmas Eve seemed a special time, between the worlds of work and family celebration. I was usually able to listen to the start of the Festival of Nine Lessons and Carols from Kings College chapel, Cambridge. The "Covid Christmas" of 2020 felt suspended in a time of darkness: restrictions, separation, loss. But we had been here before. So had He.

King's College Carols heard many times before.
Work done, damp dusk, drive home on empty roads.
Life drawing in, back, to Bethlehem.
Time out of time.

I tried to paint it once. Mary and Joseph
Backpacking east along the A158.
Signpost right to refuge, House of Bread.
Time before time.

Mood part captured. Flat fields. Bare trees. Winter sky.
Tarmac's stretch to distant dim seen wolds.
Anoraks' bright splash, defiant hope.
Time that was time.

This is not the first Christmas overtaken by
Events beyond control. Nineteen eighteen.
Empty chairs, post-war, post pandemic
Time repeats time.

Still they sing. Half willing, our masked hearts echo,
Though faintly after months of pain and grief.
Reason says "absurd". Faith whispers "hope".
Time after time.

Launching from the beach

And so I come to these last western shores
Small waves as a child's soft sleeping breath fade.
Last ripples of long ago storms that made
Unwanted change in plotted compass course
And took my ship to this now treasured source
Of joy. But I must now this place forsake.
All lands face west. All must this voyage take
No cargo more than gathered hope, remorse.

My boat is here, light oars across the thwarts,
My strength enough to run her down the beach.
Sea pebbles grate. Gentle she floats reborn.
Though I look back to shore I am now swept
By ebbing tide that takes me out of reach
Beyond the cape to dark, awaiting dawn.